BROADWAY PLAY PUBLISHING, INC.

D1038790

Babes in the Wood

by

Rick Besoyan

249 WEST 29 STREET NEW YORK NY 10001 (212) 563-3820

309

First printing: July 1983

ISBN: 0-88145-011-1

Design by Marie Donovan.
Set in Baskerville by BakerSmith Type, NYC.
Printed and bound by BookCrafters, Inc., Chelsea MI.

Time: 300 B.C. A Mid-Summer Night
Place: A Wood Near Athens

DRAMATIS PERSONAE
(In The Order in Which They Appear)

OBERON	King Of The Night
ROBIN GOODFELLOW	A Wood Sprite
TITANIA	Queen Of The Night
HELENA	An Athenian Maid
DEMETRIUS	An Athenian Youth
BOTTOM	An Athenian Weaver
LYSANDER	Another Athenian Youth
HERMIA	Another Athenian Maid

MUSICAL NUMBERS

ACT ONE

1. This State of Affairs	Oberon and Goodfellow
2. The Alphabet Song	Titania
3. A Lover Waits	Oberon
4. The Gossip Song	Helena
5. I'm Not for You	Demetrius with Helena
6. Mother	Bottom
Old Fashioned Girl	Bottom and Goodfellow
7. Love Is Lovely	Lysander and Hermia
8. Babes in the Wood	Goodfellow
Reprise—Love Is Lovely	Lysander with Helena
9. Finale—Act One	The Company

ACT TWO

1. Opening—Act Two	The Company
Cavorting	Titania and Bottom
2. There's a Girl	Oberon and Demetrius
Reprise—There's a Girl	Demetrius
3. Reprise—I'm Not for You	Lysander
4. Little Tear	Hermia
Reprise—Babes in the Wood	Goodfellow
5. Menage à Trois	Helena with Lysander and Demetrius
6. Helena	Demetrius and Lysander
7. Mid-Summer Night	Oberon and Lysander
8. Moon Madness	Titania and Bottom
9. Reprise—A Lover Waits	Oberon
Reprise—The Alphabet Song	Titania, Hermia & Helena
Finale—Act Two	The Company

ACT ONE

Music in. The curtain rises and the lights come up on a wood near Athens. OBERON, *a god of imposing stature, is discovered. Music out.*

OBERON: I, Oberon, King of the Night, return to this Athenian wood to bless all married couples and pray for their continued connubial bliss. If lovers grieve, I come to soothe their troubled souls and help untangle the skein of mortal complications.

(Music under dialogue. Calling)

Good fellow. Robin Goodfellow, your King has returned.

ROBIN GOODFELLOW, *an aged wood sprite, shuffles on looking about him.*

GOODFELLOW: Your majesty? Ah, your majesty, welcome. Welcome home. *(Helps* OBERON *remove his cape)*

OBERON: It's good to be back. But tell me, Goodfellow, how is my lovely wife, Titania?

GOODFELLOW: Oh, your majesty, she has been most anxious for your return. I might even say she's been overly anxious.

TITANIA, *a beautiful and regal goddess, enters and bows before* OBERON.

OBERON: Rise, my dear. Rise and come to my arms.

TITANIA: *(Coolly)* As your Queen I bow before you. As your wife I choose not your embrace.

OBERON: What's this, my dear?

TITANIA: Tell me, sire, how was your journey?

OBERON: Routine, my dear. Nothing but routine.

TITANIA: For you, I imagine it was. I imagine that all of your journeys include giving a token of your affection to young goddesses. For example, on this journey you gave a perfectly matched pearl necklace to an Indian goddess of doubtful reputation.

OBERON: Please, my dear, not in front of the servants. This had best be discussed in the privacy of our connubial bower.

TITANIA: There is nothing further to discuss, my lord. Until I feel you have sufficiently repented for the indignities you've forced me to suffer, I shall stay in my part of the wood. I trust you shall stay in yours.

OBERON: But, my dear . . .

TITANIA: The subject is closed.

(TITANIA *bows and exits. Music out*)

OBERON: Women, women, women. Will they never understand the noble nature of man? Tell me, Goodfellow, could I in all good conscience spurn the love of the gentle Indian goddess? Why, it might have caused her grievous mental anguish for years to come.

GOODFELLOW: You're so right, your majesty.

OBERON: Spied on me, that's what the fair Titania has done. And it's not the first time, mark you. How base. How deceitful.

GOODFELLOW: Oh, I couldn't agree more.

OBERON: But this time my Queen has gone too far. The time has come for me to take action. And, Goodfellow, you shall help me.

OBERON *and* GOODFELLOW *sing* THIS STATE OF AFFAIRS.

THIS STATE OF AFFAIRS

OBERON: This state of affairs

GOODFELLOW: This state of affairs

OBERON: Calls for action

GOODFELLOW: To war

OBERON: This state of affairs

GOODFELLOW: This state of affairs

OBERON: Calls for might

GOODFELLOW: It calls for might

OBERON: This state of affairs calls for battling the foe
    And I'm prepared to start the fight

GOODFELLOW: Let's start the fight

OBERON: It's time for a change

GOODFELLOW: It's time for a change

OBERON: For the master

GOODFELLOW: To war

OBERON: It's time for a change

GOODFELLOW: It's time for a change

OBERON: For the spouse

GOODFELLOW: Let's change the spouse

OBERON: It's time for a change to reaffirm just who I am
    If I'm a man or I'm a mouse

GOODFELLOW: You're not a mouse

OBERON: Yes, I am King of the Nighttime

GOODFELLOW: Horraw

OBERON: I won't be a King on the spot

GOODFELLOW: Get off the spot

OBERON: And I am King of the mountain

GOODFELLOW: Horraw

OBERON: That is 'til the Queen says I'm not

GOODFELLOW: Rot

OBERON: This state of affairs

GOODFELLOW: This state of affairs

OBERON: Leaves me seething

GOODFELLOW: To war

OBERON: This state of affairs

GOODFELLOW: This state of affairs

OBERON: I decry

GOODFELLOW: Yes, we decry

OBERON: This state of affairs will bring this man his rightful
    Or, dammit, I will do or die

GOODFELLOW: You will die

Music under dialogue.

GOODFELLOW: Caution, your majesty. Action should be tempered with caution, particularly where a woman is concerned.

OBERON: I toss caution to the winds, Goodfellow. This very evening I shall bewitch my Titania. Heretofore she has been invisible to human eyes, even as you and I. Tonight both man and beast shall view her fair person. Once bewitched, I shall shower her with a sprinkling of moondust and my Queen shall fall hopelessly in love with whomever she first sees.

GOODFELLOW: Oh, that's excellent, your majesty. But, begging your pardon, sire, two sprinklings of moondust are required for your wishes.

OBERON: Are you sure, Goodfellow? Two sprinklings of moondust seem rather potent.

GOODFELLOW: Oh, I'm quite certain, your majesty. Bewitchment, curses and enchantments have long been a hobby of mine.

OBERON: Then so be it. And tonight I shall have a revenge long overdue.

OBERON *and* GOODFELLOW *sing.*

OBERON: For I am the King of the lovers

GOODFELLOW: Ta-da

OBERON: I won't be King on the brink

GOODFELLOW: Ta-da-da-da

OBERON: And I am the King of the passions

GOODFELLOW: Ta-da

OBERON: So I'll tell the Queen what I think

Bronx cheer.

OBERON: This state of affairs

GOODFELLOW: Ha-ha-ha-ha-ha

OBERON: Calls for magic

GOODFELLOW: Ha-ha

OBERON: This state of affairs

GOODFELLOW: Ha-ha-ha-ha-ha

OBERON: She will rue

GOODFELLOW: Ha-ha-ha-ha-ha, Ah-ha, ah-ha, ha-ha . . .

OBERON: *(Spoken)* Goodfellow, who is your King and leader?

GOODFELLOW: *(Spoken)* Oh, you are, sire. I merely follow.

OBERON: *(Spoken)* Well, don't forget it. Come now and follow along

OBERON & GOODFELLOW: *(Sung)* This state of affairs
Will cause a wild love affair
Between the Queen and who knows who?

OBERON *and* GOODFELLOW *exit after their song. Music in and out for* TITANIA's *entrance.*

TITANIA: Does Titania, Queen of the Night, seem harsh to Oberon, her husband? Would that I could recommend similar treatment to all those mortal women who wonder why their marriages are unhappy. 'Tis but the old, old tale: the battle of the sexes. You must conquer him before he conquers you. From what I have witnessed of late, however, womanhood is fast falling into utter servitude, a state I deplore. Ah, if each and every mortal woman would only remember her childhood training, things would be different indeed.

TITANIA *sings* THE ALPHABET SONG

THE ALPHABET SONG

TITANIA: Ladies, ladies, wherever you may be
What's happened to our feminist society?
Ladies, ladies, I fear that you forget
The creed we used to love so well and learned by alphabet
        Who wears the pants in your abode?
        Let me remind you of our code:
A is for the *A*nger he will show you as you tame him
    B is for your *B*laming if his anger ever shows
C is for the Cross you bear as mentally you maim him
    That's what every woman knows

D is for *D*omesticate, speak softly to him, wait now,
    E is for your *E*ffort to explain just how it goes
F is for his *F*ailure, so you hit him with a plate now
    That's what every woman knows

        G is for his *G*ender which is wild
        H: when he feels *H*eady you feel flat
        I is for your *I*nnocence defiled

J is for he'll *J*olly pay for that
  Forevermore, and

K is for your *K*ing who is a slavey and a runt now
  L is: how you *L*ove it from your head down to your toes
M is for your *M*arriage, it is everything you want now
  That's what every woman knows
    What every woman knows

N is for your *N*agging, you must nag him every minute
  O is for your *O*pen mouth; make sure it doesn't close
P is for his *P*eace but you must never let him win it
  That's what every woman knows

Q: when treated *Q*ueenly there's adultery, he commits it
  R: he's had a *R*oving eye and wild oats he sows
S is for the *S*eizure you will have 'til he admits it
  That's what every woman knows

  T is when you tease and titillate him
    U: he's got the *U*rge but you're the boss
  V: he's on the *v*erge, then as you bait him
    Double U is for your Double Cross
      (A headache works) and

X is for *X*antippe, go to her and you'll discover
  Y is for the *Y*outh you spent to teach him and it shows
Z is for, by *Z*eus, at last you're free to take a lover
  That's what every woman knows
    What every woman knows

At the end of the song TITANIA *slowly becomes bewitched as* OBERON
sings A LOVER WAITS.

A LOVER WAITS

OBERON: *(Off-stage)* Titania, Titania,
Oberon bewitches you,
Oberon bewitches you I vow

OBERON: *(Enters)* Titania, Titania,
Oberon bewitches you,
Oberon bewitches you now:

A lover waits, a lover waits
  Alone in the night
A lover waits, a lover waits for you
    Though it may seem
    A gossamer dream
He'll lead you to joys you never knew

A lover waits, a lover waits
   The moonlight appears
Your guiding light before the night has flown
     Soon you'll be kissed
     Somewhere in the mist
Where a lover waits, a lover waits alone

Music under dialogue.

OBERON: *(Sprinkles moondust on Titania)* Listen well, Titania: you who are cold, distant and aloof to your Oberon shall this night desire love above all else. You shall find that love, Titania. Somewhere in this wood you will soon gaze on the creature of your desire. Go now and find him.

OBERON *sprinkles more moondust on* TITANIA *and* TITANIA *wanders off in a trance.* OBERON *sings.*

OBERON: A lover waits, a lover waits
   The moonlight appears
Your guiding light before the night has flown
     Soon you'll be kissed
     Somewhere in the mist
Where a lover waits, a lover waits alone

At the end of the song OBERON *disappears.* HELENA, *a perky Athenian maiden, enters.*

HELENA: Come along, dear Demetrius, do come along . . . just a little bit further into the wood.

DEMETRIUS, *a lively Athenian youth, enters.*

DEMETRIUS: Stop now, Helena. Stop now and listen. I have come along with you this far, but now I will go no farther. Come, tell me the vital information you say you have for me, or I return to Athens at once. I find the whole thing most unseemly: here I am to be married to your dearest friend on the morrow and you insist on me following you into the wood.

HELENA: Dear Demetrius, I have only done so for your own well being. I would do anything for you, dear Demetrius. *Anything*.

DEMETRIUS: Then come; give me the information.

HELENA: Just one little question first, dear Demetrius. Tell me, if Hermia, your betrothed and *my dearest friend*, were to elope with another man and she were apprehended, what would happen to her?

DEMETRIUS: Why, under Athenian law, she would be put to death.

HELENA: And suppose the man with whom she eloped were, let's say, someone like *your* dearest friend, Lysander. If he were apprehended, too, what would happen to him?

DEMETRIUS: Why, he'd be put to death, too.

HELENA: Then it's just as I thought. Poor Hermia. Poor Lysander.

DEMETRIUS: Come, what are you saying? What is this foolish talk of yours?

HELENA: Poor Demetrius.

DEMETRIUS: Out with it girl. What nonsense is this of yours?

HELENA: Well, first, dear Demetrius, I must say:

DEMETRIUS *sits on a tree stump while* HELENA *sings* THE GOSSIP SONG

THE GOSSIP SONG

HELENA: I'm not one to gossip
I'm not one to carry tales about

I'm not one to gossip
Oh, no, I'd rather have my tongue cut out

(Spoken) However:

(Sung) You know the woman of your choosing
   Is my very dearest friend
And I could only wish for both of you
   A different kind of end
And yet the truth remains, your wife-to-be
   Has heard the mating call
But it's from someone else, in fact,
   She doesn't like you much at all.

And if you have the slightest interest
   In the man who stole her heart
I really shouldn't tell you this
   But it's the really juicy part
And as I've always said, the truth will out,
   So why should we pretend?
And so the woman of your choosing
   Loves your very dearest friend

Oh, it's gone on for weeks and weeks
   And I will only tell you this
I've never seen two people so in love
   And what's more, when they kiss,
It's with such passion and such ardor
   They should really use a bed
But then I'm sure they have and, goodness me,
   Your face is turning red

And you well know the law in Athens
   And the minute you appear
They'd soon be punished and the punishment
   It seems is quite severe
I think they're drawn and then they're quartered,
   But now let me catch my breath,
Well, if it isn't that at *you* I'm sure
   They'd laugh themselves to death

And so the woman of your choosing
   And your very dearest friend

Are in the process of eloping
  And this evening they will spend
A blissful night of love together
  In this wood they'll rendezvous
So you should stab them both to death
  For it's the kindest thing to do

Oh, I'm an understanding woman
  And I know just how you feel
To kill your wife-to-be and very dearest
  Friend, but all things heal
And when this ugly mess is over
  I feel certain you'll agree
The one you really love
  Is no one else but me

At the end of the song DEMETRIUS *rises angrily.*

DEMETRIUS: Tell me, tell me, is this true?

HELENA: I swear to you, every word of it is true, poor, dear, Demetrius.

DEMETRIUS: Then you're right. I'll slay the both of them.

HELENA: Oh, that's wonderful.

DEMETRIUS: Well, at least I'll slay Lysander.

HELENA: And Hermia? You really must slay her, too.

DEMETRIUS: Slay my dear, sweet Hermia? I don't think I could do it.

HELENA: You've got to be strong. Then, at least, you'll be free to marry me.

DEMETRIUS: Marry you?

HELENA: Oh, Demetrius, how it hurts me to see you mooning over that fickle Hermia when I want you so much. Do you think I would have betrayed the confidence of my very dearest friend if I didn't love you beyond all reason? I love you, Demetrius, I love you.

DEMETRIUS: Well, I'm sorry about that, Helena, but the truth of the matter is: I don't love you.

HELENA: But I'm youthful, charming, pretty.

DEMETRIUS: That may be, but the simple fact remains, I could never marry you.

HELENA: Then we'll live in sin together. Anything!

DEMETRIUS: Poor, dear Helena, listen:

DEMETRIUS, *with* HELENA, *sings* I'M NOT FOR YOU.

I'M NOT FOR YOU

DEMETRIUS: Almost every male I know delights in females
  We males persist until a victory's won
And almost every single male I know in Athens
  Hath ends not very noble, but they're fun

  Yet every once in a special while
    With a girl you'll meet
    Who's much too sweet
    You feel discreet

  And every once in a special while
    You don't want your way
    Don't want to play
    You want to say:

  I'm no angel, I'm no devil
I'm inclined to let things go or follow through
  But there's one thing on the level
I'm not for you

  I could hurt you, I could charm you
I'm a realist with a lovely dream or two
  But there's one thing, I won't harm you
I'm not for you

    What you see in me's a riddle
      I can't understand
    I'll be playing second fiddle
      Not leading the band

When you meet him, then he'll hold you
And you'll meet him just as sure as dreams come true
   You'll remember what I told you
I'm not for you

DEMETRIUS *and* HELENA *dance: he trying to show her the impossibility of his loving her, she not convinced that he won't succumb to her charms.*

At the end of the dance OBERON *appears.*

OBERON: What's this? An Athenian maiden and youth in the wood at this time of night? As I am invisible to mortals I shall overhear their conversation.

DEMETRIUS *and* HELENA *sing.*

DEMETRIUS: What you see in me's a riddle
   I can't understand

HELENA: I do

DEMETRIUS: I'll be playing second fiddle
   Not leading the band

HELENA: It's you

DEMETRIUS: When you meet him

HELENA: I love you

DEMETRIUS: Then he'll hold you

HELENA: I love you

DEMETRIUS: And you'll meet him
   Just as sure as dreams come true

HELENA: You're the best, by far

DEMETRIUS: You'll remember

HELENA: I love you

DEMETRIUS: What I told you

HELENA: I love you

DEMETRIUS: I'm not

HELENA: Yes, you are

DEMETRIUS: For

HELENA: Yes, you are

DEMETRIUS: You.

HELENA: Yes, you are, yes, you are,
   Yes, you are, yes, you are,
      Yes, you are, yes, you are,
         Yes, you are, yes you are.

At the end of the song DEMETRIUS *and* HELENA *exit.* GOODFELLOW *enters.*

GOODFELLOW: *(Bowing)* Robin Goodfellow at your service, sire.

OBERON: Tell me, Goodfellow, have you any moondust at your disposal?

GOODFELLOW: Oh, my, yes. I always keep a goodly supply handy.

OBERON: Then search the wood for an Athenian youth and maiden. Cause them to sleep and as they are sleeping drop the moondust into the eyes of the youth. When he wakens he shall see the maid and fall madly in love with her; she, who asks desperately for that love. Then, together, they shall live happily ever after.

GOODFELLOW: What a lovely thought, sire. I go at once.

OBERON: But stay. I see yet another youth approaching. Let us see what he is about.

The lights fade on OBERON *and* GOODFELLOW *as* BOTTOM, *an elfish youth, enters rapidly.* BOTTOM *hides behind a tree, then peeps out.*

BOTTOM: There, at last. I do think I have finally rid myself of that silly, pursuing female. *(Drinks from a skin bag)*
Horrible stuff. *(Drinks again)* To think that I, Bottom, the weaver, am continually reduced to running away from all of Athen's unmarried women. *(Drinks again)* Any why should this be? Am I rich? No. The weaver's trade is scarcely a lucrative one. Am I clever? No. In all honesty I just pass being a dullard. Handsome perhaps? No. Bottom is at least wise enough to know he is on the rather plain side. Then why all this attention from the female sex? *(Drinks again)*
This is why: I am single. A single male. A single male is not safe until he is sacrificed on the altar of matrimony. If only they'd stop pursuing me. If only I could do the pursuing once, just once, all by myself. Oh, modern maidenhood, what's gotten into you?

BOTTOM *sings* MOTHER.

MOTHER

BOTTOM: Almost every single girl I've met since Mother
Had something or other
   That really didn't suit my taste

And almost every girl, since Mother cured my colic,
Has wanted to frolic
   But I'm still innocent, though chased

    For the girls of today
      I have a dreadful fear
    And if Mother only knew
      She'd see my plight

    What's become of the dainty girls
      Of yesteryear
    Oh, Oedipus Rex, you're so
      Right, right, right:

There's no one like Mother
There's no one like Mother at all
   You may find another

But she can't compare
With your sweetheart with the silver hair

Oh, Mother dear, I'm calling to you
The one you called your loving baby, divine
   There's no one, no one at all,
   Like that true blue lady
She's that wonderful Mother of mine.

After the song BOTTOM *sits and takes a swig from the skin bag.*

OBERON: Goodfellow, that boy needs help.

GOODFELLOW: Oh, I couldn't agree more, your majesty.

OBERON: There must be some way to help the lad. I have it: a brilliant idea.

GOODFELLOW: I'm sure it is, your majesty.

OBERON: We shall enchant the lad and turn him into a lion; a courageous lion.

GOODFELLOW: Oh, that's excellent.

OBERON: But, wait. I shall cause my Titania to fall asleep. You will lead our friend here to her side. When she awakens she will fall hopelessly in love with the beast. My revenge shall be complete. Now then, while I search for the fair Titania, can you enchant the lad and turn him into a lion?

GOODFELLOW: Oh, there's nothing to it. Lions have always been more or less a specialty of mine.

OBERON: Then I shall go on my mission; you on yours.

OBERON *disappears.*

GOODFELLOW: Farewell, sire, farewell. *(Crossing down to* BOTTOM*)* What a joy it is to be able to help these poor mortals. It's a pity that they can't see or hear me, however. I could give them such excellent advice.

BOTTOM: Oh, hello, there.

GOODFELLOW: What do you mean, "Hello"? You can't see me.

BOTTOM: And why not, pray tell?

GOODFELLOW: Because you're a mortal and I'm a wood sprite. Mortals can't see wood sprites. That is unless . . . *(Pointing to the skin bag)* Ah ha. Mortals can't see wood sprites unless they're under the influence of alcohol. You're drunk.

BOTTOM: And I don't even like the stuff. But I'm grieving over the loss of my mother.

GOODFELLOW: Oh, I'm sorry. When was the demise?

BOTTOM: Come October it will be sixteen years.

GOODFELLOW: Good heavens, boy, you've got to get hold of yourself. You've got to live, love, find yourself a woman.

BOTTOM: They don't make girls like Mother anymore.

GOODFELLOW: That's where you're wrong. I'm going to introduce you to the very woman of your dreams.

BOTTOM: You don't say?

GOODFELLOW: Just follow me.

BOTTOM: *(Rising)* You're sure now she's an old fashioned girl: gentle, demure, innocent?

GOODFELLOW: Indeed, yes. Oh, by the way, she's very fond of animals.

BOTTOM: Of course. She would be.

GOODFELLOW: And she's particularly fond of one who's courageous.

BOTTOM: I'm afraid that leaves me out.

GOODFELLOW: Not at all. That is, if you don't mind undergoing a small physical change. I can make you powerful and strong: a veritable lion.

BOTTOM: Oh, would you?

GOODFELLOW: Indeed, I will. And I guarantee you, once the lady sees you, you'll be a roaring success.

BOTTOM *and* GOODFELLOW *sing* OLD FASHIONED GIRL

OLD FASHIONED GIRL

BOTTOM: Give me

GOODFELLOW: I'll give you

BOTTOM & GOODFELLOW: An old fashioned girl
In an old fashioned garden for two

I'm sure that she'll serve
   An old fashioned tea
I'll (you'll) bend
   An old fashioned knee:
      Proposing

She'll blush
   Her "Yes" won't be bold
For her fashion is old
   As can be

Then I'll (you'll) say,
   "I love an old fashioned girl
Who will fashion an old fashioned me."

Music under dialogue.

BOTTOM: I can see how it will be when you introduce us. How demure. How innocent she'll be. I'll say, "how-de-do," reckless, like that. She'll pretend to be upset and she'll walk away from me. And then . . .

GOODFELLOW: Yes, yes?

BOTTOM: She'll drop her . . . hankie. I'll pick it up. And then . . .

GOODFELLOW: Yes, yes?

BOTTOM: I'm sure that she'll smile
I'll give her her hankie

GOODFELLOW: I'm sure she'll say, "thankie"
Not "merci"

Then I'll (you'll) say,
  "I love an old fashioned girl
    Who will fashion an old fashioned,
    Fashion an old fashioned,
    Fashion an old fashioned me"

After their song, BOTTOM *and* GOODFELLOW *exit.* LYSANDER, *a handsome youth and* HERMIA, *a very pretty maiden, enter. He holds her hand.*

LYSANDER: Come, dear Hermia, this is the glade. Here we shall rest until daybreak. Then, on to a city that's friendlier to lovers than Athens. There we shall be joined as man and wife.

HERMIA: What lovely words, dear Lysander, "man and wife."

LYSANDER: For all practical purposes we're already man and wife. Our honeymoon chambers shall be this wood. The starry sky shall be our coverlet, the grassy down, our bed. For this, this shall be our wedding night.

HERMIA: I beg your pardon?

LYSANDER: This shall be our wedding night.

HERMIA: Dear, dear Lysander, our joyous wedding night must wait until our marriage is a legal one.

LYSANDER: But, my only one, certainly a mere piece of paper should not withhold the desire we feel for one another.

HERMIA: Love of my life, I'm afraid it does.

LYSANDER: Sweetest of all, if you would just see it my way . . .

HERMIA: I think I'm getting a headache.

LYSANDER: Oh, dear love, your cruel Lysander has upset you. Forgive me. Of course we shall be legally married before our love is consummated.

HERMIA: Oh, Lysander, I do love you so.

LYSANDER: And I love you.

HERMIA: Now, then, where shall we rest our weary heads?

LYSANDER: Here, my love; on this soft bower we shall nestle together.

HERMIA: Thank you, dear Lysander. And you can sleep over there. *(Rests on the ground)*

LYSANDER: Yes, yes. Exactly what I had in mind. *(Rests on the ground)* Hermia?

HERMIA: Yes, Lysander?

LYSANDER *and* HERMIA *sing* LOVE IS LOVELY

LOVE IS LOVELY

LYSANDER: Love is lovely and love is dear
Loving someone who's warm and near
   Love is lovely when you feel
   All the dreams you dreamed of are real

Love is lovely when you can touch
Touching someone can mean so much
   Touching someone who'll say,
   "Stay, love is lovely in every way"

HERMIA: Love is lovely and love is dear
Loving someone who's warm and near
   Love is lovely when you feel
   All the dreams you dreamed of are real

Love is lovely when you can touch
Touching someone can mean so much
   Touching someone who'll say,
   "Stay, love is lovely in every way"

LYSANDER: We've a love that's not platonic
How delightful, how ironic
  I feel weak

HERMIA: Our love's not Aristotelian
It's more like one in a million
  Kiss my cheek

LYSANDER & HERMIA: One plus one's arithmetical
A plus B's alphabetical
Pi plus Z's hypothetical

  Let the scholars keep their canting
  We've a world that's more enchanting:

Love is lovely and love is dear
Loving someone who's warm and near

  Love is lovely when you feel
  All the dreams you dreamed of are real

Love is lovely when you can touch
Touching someone can mean so much
  Touching someone who'll say,
  "Stay, love is lovely in every way"

LYSANDER: *(Spoken)* Goodnight, Hermia.

HERMIA: *(Spoken)* Goodnight, Lysander.

LYSANDER *and* HERMIA *sleep. Music in as* GOODFELLOW *enters and crosses past the sleeping* LYSANDER. GOODFELLOW *stops, then turns back to* LYSANDER.

GOODFELLOW: Well, well, well; what a piece of good fortune. There can be no doubt that this is the very Athenian youth that my sire, Oberon, asked me to cast a love spell upon. Ah, you poor mortals. You want love more than anything in the world, yet when it comes your way, you're frightened of it.

GOODFELLOW *sings* BABES IN THE WOOD

BABES IN THE WOOD

GOODFELLOW: You're all babes in the wood
When it comes to love and romance
   You're all babes in the wood
So afraid of taking a chance

   But one searches for you alone
The night's still warm and new
      There's a moon above
      You will find your love
   A babe in the wood like you

Music under dialogue.

GOODFELLOW: *(Throws moondust in Lysander's eyes)*
There, young mortal, when the maiden who loves you so well
awakens you, you will gaze on her with new eyes: the eyes of
a lover. What unbounded happiness you will know. Ah, for
me this is all in a night's work; but what a pleasure to be in
a line of work that brings only joy to mankind.

GOODFELLOW *sings.*

   Yes, one searches for you alone
The night's still warm and new
      There's a moon above
      You will find your love
A babe in the wood like you

At the end of the song OBERON *appears.*

OBERON: Goodfellow, is that you?

GOODFELLOW: *(Crossing to* OBERON *and bowing)* Ah, your
majesty; your wish is my command.

OBERON: Obviously not. You've done it again, Goodfellow.
You've made one of your foolish errors.

GOODFELLOW: Ah, your majesty, I know just what you're going to say. It's true. I was wrong about Queen Titania and I admit it. But then, I've always said, "we all make mistakes."

OBERON: Titania? What mistake about Titania?

GOODFELLOW: You were quite right, your majesty, and I admit it. Only *one* sprinkling of moondust is to be used to bewitch someone into falling in love.

OBERON: And I used two on Titania. What will happen to her?

GOODFELLOW: Have no fears, your majesty. We might just say your Queen will be *overly* attracted to the man I turned into a roaring lion.

OBERON: A roaring lion indeed. That's the mistake to which I refer. You turned the young man into an ass.

GOODFELLOW: An ass? A hee-haw ass?

OBERON: Yes; a hee-haw ass.

GOODFELLOW: Now, how could I have managed to do that? Well, we all make mistakes, I say. Never mind, your majesty, I will rectify everything. In the meanwhile, you look yonder, sire. When the Athenian youth awakens, he will first see the maiden by his side and fall madly in love with her.

OBERON: Good heavens, Goodfellow. That's not the youth. I've never seen him before.

GOODFELLOW: But, sire, his garments *are* Athenian and he is, indeed, a youth.

OBERON: Be that as it may, he is not the one. Now go and find the correct one at once. I shall attend to my dear Titania and make sure no harm comes to her. Oh, Goodfellow, you are a sorry disappointment, indeed.

OBERON *disappears.*

GOODFELLOW: *(Exiting)* Blame. That's all I ever get, Blame.

What thanks do I receive when I'm right. None. None whatever. But just let me make one or two or three little mistakes and who gets the blame? I do. We all make mistakes now and then, I say.

GOODFELLOW *exits.* DEMETRIUS *enters, followed by* HELENA.

DEMETRIUS: Where are they? Where can they be?

HELENA: Wait, dear Demetrius. Please wait for your Helena.

DEMETRIUS: My Helena? You are *not* my Helena. Haven't I made that perfectly clear? I don't wish to offend you, Helena, but your entire being, charming though it may be, leaves me utterly cold. No; I'm in love with Hermia, make no mistake. My love for her is deep, warm, enduring. And if she won't accept it, I'll kill her. I'll kill Lysander, too. How dare my best friend take her away from me. But then that's like him. He always was the selfish one.

HELENA: Poor Demetrius.

DEMETRIUS: No pity, please. Go back to Athens and leave me in peace to continue my grim search.

HELENA: Don't be cruel, Demetrius. Just let me follow you at a respectful distance.

DEMETRIUS: Go back to Athens. Stay where you are. But leave me alone. I can speak no plainer.

DEMETRIUS *exits.*

HELENA: But, Demitrius, I love you. I love you. I love you!

LYSANDER: *(Awakening and gazing at* HELENA*)* You love me and I, I love you!

HELENA: Lysander!

LYSANDER: *(Crossing to* HELENA*)* Yes. Helena. It is your Lysander. Oh, I know you thought I loved Hermia. Perhaps I did.

But, oh, what a foolish puppy love that was. Yes, now it is you who fills me with a passion beyond all reason. It is you I love. You, dear, dear Helena.

HELENA: You must be jesting.

LYSANDER: Helena, a man in love never jests.

LYSANDER *with* HELENA, *sings* REPRISE—LOVE IS LOVELY

REPRISE—LOVE IS LOVELY

LYSANDER: Love is lovely and love is dear
Loving someone who's warm and near
    Love is lovely when you feel
All the dreams you dreamed of are real

Love is lovely when you can touch
Touching someone can mean so much
    Touching someone who'll say,
    "Stay, love is lovely in every way"

HELENA: *(Spoken)* We've been friends for a long time, Lysander; so under the circumstances:

(Sung) I'll forget your odd behavior
Say you're sorry that you gave your
    Love to me

LYSANDER: I'm not sorry, I won't say it
I've a heart, I must obey it
    Hear my plea: You can love me, I know you can

HELENA: I'm in love with another man

LYSANDER: No, you're not, I've another plan
Can't you see the love light gleaming?

HELENA: One more step and I'll start screaming!

LYSANDER: Love is lovely when you can touch

HELENA: Don't touch me

LYSANDER: Touching someone can mean so much

HELENA: Don't touch me

LYSANDER: Touching someone who'll say . . .

HELENA: Stay where you are . . .

Music out.

LYSANDER: How can you be so cruel? I love you. I love you. I love you!

HERMIA: *(Waking)* Lysander, is that you? Lysander?

LYSANDER: Don't bother me. I'm busy.

DEMETRIUS *enters.* HELENA *crosses to him.*

HELENA: Dear, Demetrius.

DEMETRIUS: Don't bother me. I'm busy. Hermia, I shouldn't forgive you but I can't help myself. I love you.

HERMIA: *(Crossing to* LYSANDER) Well, I'm sorry; but the truth is: I'm in love with Lysander.

LYSANDER: Oh, don't bother yourself about that. I'm in love with Helena.

HELENA: Demetrius!

THE COMPANY *sings,* FINALE, ACT ONE.

FINALE, ACT ONE

HELENA: I love you, I love you,
With all my heart I love you,
With all my heart I love you,
   And I don't love you

DEMETRIUS: I love you, I love you,
With all my heart I love you,
With all my heart I love you
   And I don't love you

HERMIA: I love you, I love you,
With all my heart I love you,
With all my heart I love you,
  And I don't love you

LYSANDER: I love you, I love you,
With all my heart I love you,
With all my heart I love you,
  And I don't love you

OBERON *and* GOODFELLOW *enter to see* BOTTOM, *now turned into
an ass, gallop on stage. (It is essential that* BOTTOM *be a fourlegged
ass; that is, another actor play his second half. While his face should
look as much like an ass as possible, a mask should not be used.) He
is followed by* TITANIA. TITANIA *sings:*

TITANIA: I love you, I love you,
With all my heart I love you,
With all my heart I love you,
  And I love you true

BOTTOM: You love me, you love me,
With all your heart you love me,
With all your heart you love me,
  But you're forward, too.

THE COMPANY: Strange things happen in mid-Summer,
Happen in mid-Summer
  Happen in the night

Strange things happen in mid-Summer,
Happen in mid-Summer,
  'Neath a starry light

Strange things,
Who can understand?
  Strange things
Who will take my hand?
Strange things,
  Who is in command?:

Some wicked old god
With a humor that's odd
  Or it could be instead
  He's not well in the head
But whatever it is
It's no time for a quiz

I can only hope and trust
  All will be right
  By dawn's early light

Strange things are straightened out
  Strange things will be straightened out
    That happen on a mid-Summer night

For no one searches for me alone
  And no one hears my plea:
    There's a moon above
    I have lost my love
  So who is the babe in the wood for me?

THE CURTAIN FALLS

ACT TWO

Music in. At curtain's rise OBERON *and* GOODFELLOW *are disco-vered. Also discovered, but in darkness and in "frozen" positions, are* HELENA, HERMIA, DEMETRIUS *and* LYSANDER. *Music out as* OBE-RON *speaks the following poem:*

OBERON: How confusing the proceedings
What a complicated plot
  Something's happened to my planning
Something's happened that should not

I'm a god with many powers
So in melody and rhyme
  We'll review the past proceedings
For I'll turn back . . . time

The lights come up on HELENA, HERMIA, DEMETRIUS *and* LYSAN-DER. OPENING, ACT TWO.

OPENING, ACT TWO

HELENA: I love you, I love you,
With all my heart I love you,
With all my heart I love you,
  And I don't love you

DEMETRIUS: I love you, I love you
With all my heart I love you,
With all my heart I love you,
  And I don't love you

HERMIA: I love you, I love you,
With all my heart I love you,
With all my heart I love you,
  And I don't love you

LYSANDER: I love you, I love you
With all my heart I love you,
With all my heart I love you,
    And I don't love you

BOTTOM, *as the ass, gallops on stage. He is followed by* TITANIA.
TITANIA *sings:*

I love you, I love you,
With all my heart I love you,
With all my heart I love you,
    And I love you true

BOTTOM: You love me, you love me
With all your heart you love me,
With all your heart you love me,
But you're forward, too

THE COMPANY: Strange things happen in mid-Summer
Happen in mid-Summer
    Happen in the night

Strange things happen in mid-Summer
Happen in mid-Summer
    'Neath a starry light

Strange things,
Who can understand?
    Strange things,
    Who is in command?

Some wicked old god
With a humor that's odd
    Or it could be instead
    He's not well in the head
But whatever it is
It's no time for a quiz

I can only hope and trust
All will be right
By Dawn's early light

Strange things are straightened out
Strange things will be straightened out
  That happen on a mid-Summer night

For no one searches for me alone
And no one hears my plea:
  There's a moon above
  I have lost my love
So who is the babe in the wood for me?

After OPENING, ACT TWO, Bottom *brays.*

BOTTOM: Good heavens. What was that?

TITANIA: *(Putting an arm around* BOTTOM's *neck)* Only the
sound of your sweet voice.

BOTTOM: Aggressive women. I can't stand aggressive women.
(BOTTOM *gallops off)*

TITANIA: Wait. Wait for your Titania. (TITANIA *exits)*

HERMIA: *(Taking* LYSANDER's *arm)* Dear, Lysander. What has
come over you?

LYSANDER: It should be very clear. I'm in love with Helena.
And I'll thank you not to touch me.

HERMIA: How . . . how could you treat me this way? *(An an-
guished* HERMIA *exits)*

DEMETRIUS: Wait, dear Hermia, I'll take care of you. *(To*
HELENA) Don't touch me. *(Exiting)* Wait, Hermia, I love you.
I forgive you. I forgive you. It's all Lysander's fault. (DEMET-
RIUS *exits)*

HELENA: *(To* LYSANDER) Will you keep your hands off me.
(Exiting) Wait, Demetrius. Don't leave me alone with this sex
fiend. Demetrius, wait. (HELENA *exits)*

LYSANDER: *(Exiting)* Helena, don't leave. I want to talk to you.
I want to hold you. I want to make love to you. Helena.
(LYSANDER *exits)*

OBERON: Well, you certainly botched up this job. I trust my dear Titania will be safe while I untangle this mess you've made.

GOODFELLOW: Oh, perfectly safe.

OBERON: Then if you won't find it too inconvenient you might try to help me find the youths. (OBERON *disappears*)

GOODFELLOW: *(Exiting)* Oh, it's all well and good when things are going according to plan. He takes all the credit. But let a little something go wrong and who gets blamed? Poor, old Robin Goodfellow, that's who. I ought to quit, that's what I ought to do. He'd be sorry then.

GOODFELLOW *exits.* BOTTOM *trots on and sits. He rises as* TITANIA *enters.*

BOTTOM: Oh, it's you again.

TITANIA: *(Throwing her arms around* BOTTOM's *neck)* Yes, my darling and I love you.

BOTTOM: *(Walking away)* I told you, I can't stand aggressive women.

TITANIA: Don't scold your Titania. I will be anything you wish. If you like your women weak, insignificant, snivelling then so it shall be. Come; let us frolic together. Let us dance.

BOTTOM: There: see how you are? If I wish to dance *I* shall ask you. *(Brays)* There's that noise again. Well, I shall dance with you, on trail, so to speak. But I must *lead* and you must follow.

TITANIA: I'll try to follow. With all my heart I'll try.

BOTTOM: I suggest you do; because if you don't, I'll feel obliged to give you a good . . . *(Brays)* kick.

BOTTOM *and* TITANIA *do* CAVORTING, *a dance. It starts out slowly at first with* BOTTOM *leading.* TITANIA *becomes more aggressive as the music becomes faster and faster. At the end of the dance*

TITANIA *frightens* BOTTOM *and he gallops off-stage with* TITANIA *in hot pursuit.*

After the dance OBERON *appears.* DEMETRIUS *enters.*

DEMETRIUS: *(Calling)* Hermia. Oh, Hermia.

OBERON: Ah; here is one of the Athenians for whom I search.

DEMETRIUS: *(Calling)* Hermia. (OBERON *comes down to* DEMETRIUS) Where can she have gone? I fear for her safety in this wood.

OBERON: I could use a sprinkling of moondust to direct his love to the proper maiden but I prefer to try an experiment. Even though he can neither see nor hear me I shall use my power as a god to transfer my wishes to him.

OBERON *and* DEMETRIUS *sing* THERE'S A GIRL

THERE'S A GIRL

OBERON: *(Spoken)* There's a girl known as Helena who has every quality a man could possibly wish for: beauty, charm, grace and warmth; tenderness and loving kindness and furthermore she could make a man happy all his life.

OBERON: *(Sung)* What does this prove?

DEMETRIUS: *(Sung)* She'd make someone else a good wife

OBERON: *(Spoken)* On the other hand there's a girl known as Hermia who has every quality to make a man unhappy. Foolish, mean, deceitful and worst of all she's plain and unattractive and to compare her to Helena is like casting swine before pearls.

OBERON: *(Sung)* What does this prove?

DEMETRIUS: *(Sung)* I like ugly girls

OBERON *throws moondust on* DEMETRIUS.

OBERON: *(Sung)* Wait now, wait now, can't you see it?

DEMETRIUS: *(Sung)* Wait now, wait now, I can see it:

DEMETRIUS: *(Spoken)* It's Helena; Yes, it's Helena!

The rest of the song is sung.

OBERON: There's a girl who thinks you're wonderful

DEMETRIUS: There's a girl who thinks I'm wonderful

OBERON: There's a girl who thinks you're marvelous

DEMETRIUS: There's a girl who thinks I'm marvelous

OBERON: There's a girl, the perfect girl for you

DEMETRIUS: For me

OBERON: She loves you, how wise

DEMETRIUS: How wise

OBERON: How clever

DEMETRIUS: How clever

OBERON: She will have your love

DEMETRIUS: My love

OBERON: Forever

DEMETRIUS: Forever

OBERON: There'll be skies of blue to share with her

DEMETRIUS: There'll be skies of blue to share with her

OBERON: If it rains then you'll be there with her

DEMETRIUS: If it rains then I'll be there with her

OBERON & DEMETRIUS: With the girl who suits you (me) to a "T"

DEMETRIUS: Gee, there's a girl, she's simply wonderful

OBERON: Keep repeating, "simply wonderful"

OBERON & DEMETRIUS: "There's a girl, a girl for me"

OBERON *disappears as* DEMETRIUS *sings* REPRISE—THERE'S A GIRL

REPRISE—THERE'S A GIRL

DEMETRIUS: I can see it now,
I see it now,
 I see it oh, so clearly

I see it now,
I see it now,
 The one I love so dearly:

I'm in love with Helena,
I'm in love with Helena,
 I'm in love with Helena:
  She's the girl for me

There's a girl who thinks I'm wonderful
There's a girl who thinks I'm marvelous
 There's a girl, the perfect girl for me
  She loves me; how wise, how clever:
  She will have my love forever

There'll be skies of blue to share with her
If it rains then I'll be there with her
 With the girl who suits me to "T"

Gee, there's a girl, she's simply wonderful
There's a girl, she's simply marvelous
 There's a girl, a girl for me

DEMETRIUS *does an exuberant dance. Then:*

There'll be blue skies to share with her
If it rains then I'll be there with her
 With the girl who suits me to a "T"

Gee, there's a girl, she's simply wonderful

There's a girl, she's simply marvelous
  There's a girl, a girl for me

DEMETRIUS *dances off at the end of the song.* LYSANDER, *followed by* HERMIA, *enters.*

LYSANDER: *(Calling)* Helena. Oh, Helena.

HERMIA: Please, dear Lysander, please hear what I have to say to you.

LYSANDER: There's nothing for you to say, Hermia. It's a simple fact: I'm in love with Helena.

HERMIA: But you love me. I know you love me.

LYSANDER: I admit, I did love you, but all that seems so long ago. I now give my heart to my one true love, Helena. I do hope I haven't caused you any inconvenience.

HERMIA: Inconvenience?

LYSANDER: One day we might even be friends. But knowing your feeling for me at this time, I think it best that we not see one another for awhile. Don't worry, you'll get over me. You see, your love for me is really only puppy love.

LYSANDER *sings* REPRISE—I'M NOT FOR YOU.

REPRISE—I'M NOT FOR YOU

LYSANDER: Go away, go away little girl
Please go away from me
  Run along and play little girl
    Little girl can't you see:

I'm no angel, I'm no devil
I'm inclined to let things go or follow through
  But there's one thing on the level
I'm not for you

I could hurt you, I could charm you
I'm a realist with a lovely dream or two

But there's one thing, I won't harm you
I'm not for you
   What you see in me's a riddle
      I can't understand
   I'll be playing second fiddle
      Not leading the band

When you meet him, then he'll hold you
And you'll meet him just as sure as dreams come true
   You'll remember what I told you, so,

Run along and play little girl
   Little girl can't you see?
 Go away, go away little girl
   Please go away from me

After the song the following is sung as a bridge between REPRISE—
I'M NOT FOR YOU *and* LITTLE TEAR.

LYSANDER: What I saw in you's a riddle
I can't understand
   Now you're playing second fiddle
Not leading the band

HERMIA: But I loved you when I met you
Then you held me and my dearest dreams came true

(LYSANDER *exits without* HERMIA's *knowledge*) You can't ask me
to forget you and say, I'm not for . . .

HERMIA *turns and discovers* LYSANDER *has left her.* HERMIA *sings*
LITTLE TEAR

LITTLE TEAR

HERMIA: How revolting, how disgusting,
I was foolish, I was trusting,
   I was silly, I was simple, I was rash

How debasing, how depressing,
When the man I was caressing
   Turns and casts me out like some old bag of trash

Let her have him, let her take him
Then I hope that she'll forsake him
   Though it's touch and go with him, but mostly touch

If I wanted I could thrill him,
I could kiss him, I could kill him—
   I'm so glad it doesn't matter all that much

I should have seen his fickle way
And known his twisted mind
My time will come, I'll make him pay
   And furthermore I find . . .
      I find, I find:

Little tear, little tear
When did you arrive?
   Scarcely knew you were here
Will you grow and thrive?

Lonely tear, lonely tear
There's no need to hide
   Why pretend? You've a friend
On the other side

I'm so lucky I'll forget him
He could hurt me if I let him
   Though a man like that could never break my heart

Let him hold her, let him love 'er
I'm so grateful to discover
   Just the kind of man he was right from the start

Let him go off with another
I've a mind to tell his mother
   But I'm sure the poor old thing's already learnt

He's a cad, he's bad intention,
He's a something I can't mention:
   I won't say his folks weren't married, but they weren't

Tomorrow is a brighter day
He's not the man I'll miss
   When new horizions come my way
      And furthermore . . . What's this?
     What's this? What's this?

Little tear, little tear
  When did you arrive?
Scarcely knew you were here
  Will you grow and thrive?

Lonely tear, lonely tear
  There's no need to hide
Little tear, you've a peer
  On the other side

After the song GOODFELLOW *enters. Music under dialogue.*

GOODFELLOW: Well, well, well; what have we here? Why, it's
one of the Athenian maidens and in distress. It's a pity she
can't hear me. What words of comfort I could give her. Poor
little mortal. If only you knew that the love of your life will
soon be returned to your side.

GOODFELLOW *sings* REPRISE—BABES IN THE WOOD

REPRISE—BABES IN THE WOOD

GOODFELLOW: You're all babes in the wood
When it comes to love and romance
  You're all babes in the wood
So afraid of taking a chance

But one searches for you alone
The night's still warm and new
  There's a moon above
  You will find your love
A babe in the wood like you

HERMIA *and* GOODFELLOW *now sing their individual songs in
counterpoint:*

HERMIA:	GOODFELLOW:
Little tear, little tear	You're all babes
When did you arrive?	In the wood

When it comes to
Love and romance
Scarcely knew you were here   You're all babes
Will you grow and thrive?   In the wood
So afraid of
Taking a chance

Lonely tear, lonely tear   But one searches
There's no need to hide   For you alone
Why pretend? You've a friend   The night's still
On the other side   Warm and new
There's a moon above
You will find your love
A babe in the wood
Like you

HERMIA, *followed by* GOODFELLOW, *exits at the end of the duet.*
HELENA *backs in, followed by* LYSANDER.

HELENA: Will you stop following me about. You frighten me.
(Calling) Demetrius. Oh, Demetrius.

LYSANDER: I swear, I mean you no harm. Only listen to my
plea, but for one moment.

HELENA: Have your say then, but keep your distance.

LYSANDER: Helena, stop and consider. Do you really think
you'll ever receive the love from Demetrius you say you so
strongly desire?

HELENA: Well, I must admit; I've tried just about every wile
a woman can use.

LYSANDER: Exactly so. Then why not turn those charms on
someone who will appreciate them. Look at me, Helena. Look
at me in a different light. I don't want to brag, but am I not
a relatively attractive youth? Notice my hair, my eyes, this
chin. Is there really anything wrong with these arms, these
legs, this chest?

HELENA: I think I'm beginning to see your point.

LYSANDER: Can't you love me a little bit?

HELENA: Well, Lysander, I've always liked you. Loving you just never occurred to me. But the more I gaze on you . . . I suppose I could learn to love you.

LYSANDER: Oh, dearest one, it's foolish even to speak of such things, but I shall soon be coming into my inheritance; and I shall be very rich.

HELENA: Lysander, I love you.

LYSANDER: My darling.

As LYSANDER *and* HELENA *embrace,* DEMETRIUS *enters and separates them.*

DEMETRIUS: Unhand her, you fiend. My darling, I heard you call for help. Forgive your Demetrius. I've seen the light. I love you.

HELENA: You what?

DEMETRIUS: I love you.

HELENA: Well, that's very nice, Demetrius, but I'm afraid I've just told Lysander that I love him.

DEMETRIUS: Can you stand there and tell me you don't love me?

HELENA: Well, no. I love you, too.

DEMETRIUS: *(Taking out a dagger)* Then one of us must go.

LYSANDER: *(Taking out a dagger)* That suits me fine.

HELENA: Please, please. No bloodshed. Put your daggers away. (DEMETRIUS *and* LYSANDER *reluctantly do so*) There must be a solution. Wait!

HELENA, *with* DEMETRIUS *and* LYSANDER *sings* MENAGE A TROIS.

MENAGE A TROIS

(HELENA *with* DEMETRIUS *and* LYSANDER)

HELENA: I've got it,
I've got the solution

DEMETRIUS & LYSANDER: You have?

HELENA: I've got it
I've got the solution

DEMETRIUS & LYSANDER: You have?

HELENA: I've got it,
I've got the solution

DEMETRIUS & LYSANDER: You've told us that
Now tell us what it is

HELENA: I hear that far away they have a native dance
Though it's a bit bizarre let's give the dance a chance
For it could solve our tête-à-tête-à-tête romance
   It's called The Menage A Trois

The three of us can dance away in sheer delight
The form is fancy free with fancy taking flight
There isn't any front or back or left or right
   Let's do The Menage A Trois

Hold me, one of you hold me
One step leads to another one
   Hold me, one of you hold me
      While I hold on to the other one

They tell me once you do it you will not forget
It's in the all together once your feet get wet
   So let's begin and I'll be lucky Pierrette
   Let's do The Menage A Trois

HELENA, DEMETRIUS *and* LYSANDER *dance* THE MENAGE A
TROIS. *After the dance:*

HELENA: Hold me,

DEMETRIUS & LYSANDER: No, no

HELENA: Both of you hold me:
I won't have one of you lurking near
  Hold me,

DEMETRIUS & LYSANDER: No, no

HELENA: Both of you hold me
You know something? Something isn't working here
  Perhaps we'll learn to master it another night

DEMETRIUS & LYSANDER: No, no

HELENA: Perhaps we'll do it better in the morning light

DEMETRIUS & LYSANDER: No, no

HELENA: As Mother always said, "That's nice, you musn't fight"
Let's do The Menage A Trois

DEMETRIUS & LYSANDER: No, no

HELENA: It's called The Menage . . .

DEMETRIUS & LYSANDER: Call off The Menage

HELENA, DEMETRIUS & LYSANDER: We won't do The Menage A Trois

(Spoken) Ho-lay!!

HELENA: Well, I've certainly done the best I can. You boys will have to find your own solution.

DEMETRIUS: *(Taking out his dagger)* Then it's a duel.

LYSANDER: *(Taking out his dagger)* To the death.

HELENA: Please, not in front of me. I can't stand the sight of blood. *(Starts to leave; then turns back)* Now you boys have to promise: only one of you can get killed. Goodbye, darling. Goodbye, angel. And may the best man win me.

HELENA *exits.* DEMETRIUS *and* LYSANDER *put away their daggers, shake hands and sing:* HELENA

HELENA

DEMETRIUS & LYSANDER: Goodbye, old dear friend,
Goodbye, my dear old friend, I hope you'll have fond mem'ries
of our past;
    Will you?

Goodbye, old friend,
Goodbye, my dear old friend,
   How sad to think what I must do at last:
    Kill you

For I'm in love with Helena
She's for me
   I'm in love with Helena
    She's the key
So all my castles in the air I'd level
For just one slice of life with her, I'd revel
    That devil

But if I told my Helena
I'm too shy
   I would sure be tellin' a
    Bold faced lie
I'm on my best behavior,
    I'll toe the line
    'Til I make Helena mine

I'm in love with Helena
She's so sweet
   I'm in love with Helena
    She's complete
In clothes you're certain that she isn't neuter
   But even more, her birthday suit would suit 'er
    Cuter

And if a babe is Helena
In the woods
   I sure would be sellin' a
    Bill of goods
But still it's best behavior

And toe the line
  'Til I make Helena mine

I'm in love with Helena
She's the one
  I'm in love with Helena
    Oh, what fun
It's right to say she fires my ambition:
  Each night with her I'd like to play physician,
    Some mission

I can't describe my Helena,
Lack-a-day
  How's this? She'd look well in a
    Stack o'hay
But still it's best behavior
  And toe the line
    'Til I make my Helena mine
      'Til I make my Helena mine
        'Til I make my Helena mine

After the song DEMETRIUS *and* LYSANDER *exit.* OBERON *appears.*

OBERON: *(Calling)* Goodfellow. Robin Goodfellow.

GOODFELLOW: *(Entering and bowing)* Coming, sire. I'm coming. Ah, yes. Robin Goodfellow at your service.

OBERON: Goodfellow, where have you been?

GOODFELLOW: Oh, your majesty, you'll be pleased. I found one of the Athenian maidens you asked me to look for. I haven't taken my eyes off the poor thing.

OBERON: Your orders were to look for the men. I've taken care of one of them but now they're about to do battle to the death over one of the maids. Aren't you ashamed of yourself?

GOODFELLOW: Well, sire, I can't be expected to do everything. I could point out that if you hired enough help this kind of thing wouldn't happen.

OBERON: That will be enough, Goodfellow. I shall take care of the youths. Do you think you can handle the man who was supposed to be a lion but who you turned into an ass by mistake? My poor Titania has suffered enough humiliation. Daylight is fast approaching and our deeds must be accomplished before sunrise.

GOODFELLOW: Then on to my mission. Ah, begging your pardon, sire, just what did you want me to do with the ass?

OBERON: Turn him back into a man. Then cause him to forget his adventures yet, in the recesses of his mind, let him have a vague memory of his frolic. We'll make a man of him yet.

GOODFELLOW: Indeed we will, sire.

OBERON: Do you think you can accomplish this without any errors?

GOODFELLOW: Oh, it's a most simple feat. I shall search for him at once.

OBERON: I saw my Titania and the ass cavorting near the mimosa grove but a few minutes ago.

GOODFELLOW: Excellent, your majesty. I go. *(Starts to exit)*

OBERON: Oh, Goodfellow.

GOODFELLOW: Yes, your majesty?

OBERON: The mimosa grove is this way.

GOODFELLOW: Hmm? Why, so it is. Thank you, your majesty. Thank you very much.

GOODFELLOW *exits*.

OBERON: And now to deal with the other Athenian youth.

(Music in under dialogue) From Athens there is a youth known as Lysander. Lysander, Oberon, King of the night, calls to you. (LYSANDER *enters in a trance*) Come forth, Lysander. Come forth and receive my message. Store this message in the

deepest part of your heart, for if you do, you shall love your Hermia for all the days of your life.

OBERON *and* LYSANDER *sing* MID-SUMMER NIGHT

MID-SUMMER NIGHT

OBERON & LYSANDER: Strange things happen in mid-Summer,
Happen in mid-Summer,
  Happen in the night

Strange things happen in mid-Summer
Happen in mid-Summer
  'Neath a starry light

Strange things: who can comprehend?
Strange things: lover turned to friend
Strange things: truth and fancy blend

Forget all those fancies in flight
Forget those fancies,
  Forget those fancies,
That happen on a mid-Summer night

At the end of the song OBERON *and* LYSANDER *disappear.* BOTTOM *trots on followed by* TITANIA.

BOTTOM: *(Sitting)* There now, let us rest a moment. This romp has put me out of breath. *(Brays)* Good heavens, I must be coming down with a cold.

TITANIA: Dear, dear Friend, one more frolic; then a light refreshment.

BOTTOM: I declare, I could use a bite to eat.

TITANIA: And then to bed in my flower bower. But first, our romp.

BOTTOM: There you go again: telling me what to do.

TITANIA: Do forgive your Titania. It may take a little while, but be patient with me. For with you here, I feel my whole perspective has changed.

TITANIA *and* BOTTOM *sing* MOON MADNESS

MOON MADNESS

TITANIA: I feel like kicking up my heels
And flying to the moon

BOTTOM: I feel more like an ass who wants to bray

TITANIA: I feel if you would chase me
You would catch me very soon

BOTTOM: I feel that you should run along; I'll stay

TITANIA: I feel just like a girl again
Because you're such a treat

BOTTOM: You musn't shout, my hearing's very clear

TITANIA: I feel this is our wedding night
And this our bridal suite

BOTTOM: Don't use a word like bridle when I'm near

TITANIA & BOTTOM: Goodness gracious me, oh, my
What's become of me?
    There's a moon up in the sky
Now, at last, I see:

It must be Moon Madness, Moon Madness,
What's come over me as far as I can tell
    Is Moon Madness, Moon Madness
I'm cavorting in its magic spell

TITANIA: I've been picking daisies,
How I love to greet 'em

BOTTOM: You keep picking daisies
How I love to eat 'em

TITANIA & BOTTOM: Moon Madness, Moon Madness,
What's come over us as far as I can see
    Is Moon Madness, Moon Madness,
Come and share my madness with me

TITANIA: I feel that we were meant
For one another all the while

BOTTOM: I feel that I have finally met my match

TITANIA: I feel you brimming over
With such wisdom and such guile

BOTTOM: I feel I've got an itch, so kindly scratch

TITANIA: I feel just like a butterfly
That's feeling oh, so gay

BOTTOM: I feel more like some grass I'd like to crop

TITANIA: I feel just like a babbling brook
That always wants to play

BOTTOM: I feel more like a bucketful of slop

TITANIA & BOTTOM: Goodness gracious, such a sight;
We've been put upon
    Dawn's not breaking, there's no light
So the light begins to dawn

Who cares? It's Moon Madness, Moon Madness
    What's come over me as far as I can tell
Is Moon Madness, Moon Madness
    I'm cavorting in its magic spell

TITANIA: I've a bit of sugar
And it may delight you

BOTTOM: Hold your hand out flat
Or I'm afraid I'll bite you

TITANIA & BOTTOM: Moon Madness, Moon Madness
What's come over us as far as I can see
    Is Moon Madness, Moon Madness
Come and share my madness with me

You'll love it: Moon Madness, Moon Madness
    What's come over us as far as I can see
Is Moon Madness, Moon Madness
    Come and share my madness with me

At the end of the song TITANIA *jumps on* BOTTOM's *back and rides out in triumph.* OBERON *sings off-stage.*

REPRISE—A LOVER WAITS

OBERON: Titania, Titania, Oberon is calling you,
Oberon is calling you, I vow

(OBERON *appears*)

Titania, Titania, Oberon is calling you
    Oberon is calling you, now:

Your husband waits, your husband waits,
    Alone in the night
Your husband waits, your husband waits for you
    Though it may seem
    A gossamer dream
What's happened this night is really true

TITANIA *enters and crosses to* OBERON's *side.*

OBERON: Your husband waits, your husband waits,
His arms open wide
    We'll share delight before the night has flown
        Soon comes the dawn
        And soon we'll be gone
    So a lover waits, your lover waits alone

Music under dialogue.

TITANIA: Dear husband, I feel as if I had been in a trance. Or was it but an unpleasant dream I had? Oh, what a comfort to have you by my side.

OBERON: This night will fade from your memory only so long as you remain the dutiful wife I love so well.

TITANIA: Forevermore.

OBERON: Your enchantment fades quickly. In few moments mortals will see you no more. Two Athenian maidens come to do feminine battle. Assure them that the men of their choice will soon be theirs. Then return to my side and together we shall bid farewell to this mid-Summer night.

HERMIA *and* HELENA *enter from opposite sides of the stage.*

HERMIA: Oh, there you are, you man stealer.

HELENA: Why blame me when it's your own feminine charms which are at fault.

HERMIA: You dare speak such words to me?

HELENA: It's well known: the truth hurts.

HERMIA *and* HELENA *circle each other.*

TITANIA: My husband, I go. Ladies, stop!

OBERON *disappears as* TITANIA *comes down to* HERMIA *and* HELENA *singing.* TITANIA, HERMIA *and* HELENA *sing.*

REPRISE—THE ALPHABET SONG

TITANIA: Ladies, ladies, don't play the angry shrew
A husband waits, a husband waits
　　For each of you

Ladies, ladies, I hope you won't forget
　　The rules a woman ought to know
And learns by alphabet

Who wears the pants, tell me, which spouse?

HELENA: *(Spoken)* Dear Demetrius

HERMIA: *(Spoken)* Lysander, of course

TITANIA: *(Sung)* Then you've got a home and not a house

TITANIA, HELENA & HERMIA: *A* is for his *A*rdor; to make sure it's not corrosive
　　B is for your *B*est, make sure your ardor also shows

C: the *C*ombination could be pleasantly explosive
   That's what every woman knows

D is for *D*iscovery, though at first it may seem daring
   E is for your *E*ffort to make sure the love light glows
F is for your *F*ailure if you try just "laissez-faire-ing"
   That's what every woman knows

TITANIA: *G* is for his *G*ender; you'll be bossed now

HLENA: *H*: let's have a *H*earty cheer for that

HERMIA: *I* is for the *I*nnocence you've lost now

ALL: *J*: it's just a jolly tit for tat
   (Enjoy yourself) and

K is for your *K*ing you've learned to find him strong and regal
   L is how you'll *L*ove him from his head down to his toes
M is for your *M*arriage; how delightful that it's legal
   That's what every woman knows
      What every woman knows
N is for his *N*apping, but please wake him should you need him

O is for his *O*pen eyes, just find the proper pose
   P is for his *P*eace and you can only say, "God speed him"
      That's what every woman knows

Q: when treated *Q*ueenly, is he stepping out? Well, maybe
   R: he's had a *R*oving eye, pretend that no one knows
S: he'll *S*ettle back; you just present him with a baby
      That's what every baby knows

TITANIA: *T*: when he feels *T*esty kiss him gently

HELENA: *U*: although you've got the *U*rge to kill

HERMIA: *V*: just *V*aguely whisper sentiment'ly

ALL: *Double U*: "Let's double up"; he will
   (Works miracles) and

X is for *X*antippe, what a marriage, what disaster
   Y is for your *Y*ielding, woman reaps what woman sows
Z is for, by Zeus, it's nice to have a lord and master

That's what every woman knows
  What every woman knows

At the end of the song OBERON *and* GOODFELLOW *appear.* TITANIA
joins OBERON. LYSANDER *and* DEMETRIUS *enter from either side
of the stage and join* HERMIA *and* HELENA.

LYSANDER: My Hermia; it's always really been you.

DEMETRIUS: My Helena; it's always really been you.

The two couples embrace.

OBERON: Well, my dear, it looks as if everyone will live happily
ever after. But stay. One is missing. Goodfellow, did you do
as I told you? Where is the other Athenian?

GOODFELLOW: Oh, have no fears, your majesty. Here he comes
now.

A bewildered BOTTOM *enters in the costume of a gorilla beating his
chest.*

OBERON: Good heavens, Goodfellow, you've done it again!

BOTTOM *removes his gorilla headpiece as he joins* THE COMPANY
in FINALE—ACT TWO.

FINALE—ACT TWO

Love is lovely and love is dear
Loving someone who's warm and near
  Love is lovely when you feel
  All the dreams you dreamed of are real

Love is lovely when you can touch
Touching someone can mean so much
  Touching someone who'll say,
  "Stay, love is lovely in every way"

For we're all Babes in The Wood
  When it comes to love and Romance
We're all Babes In The Wood
  So afraid of taking a chance

Yet one searches for you alone
  Let all your hopes be bright
    There's a moon above
    You will find your love
So we bow and we bid you a fond goodnight

THE CURTAIN FALLS

Curtain calls. THE COMPANY *bows. Individual bows should be in this order:* GOODFELLOW, OBERON, TITANIA, LYSANDER, HERMIA, DEMETRIUS, HELENA *and* BOTTOM. BOTTOM *then welcomes his other half, as the ass, for a bow.* THE COMPANY *bows again.*

END OF OPERA

SOME RAIN

by James Edward Luczak

Set in rural Alabama in 1968, the play is the bittersweet tale of a middle-aged waitress whose ability to love and be loved is re-kindled by her chance encounter with a young drifter. First presented in 1982 at the Eugene O'Neill Playwright's Conference and Off-Broadway on Theatre Row.

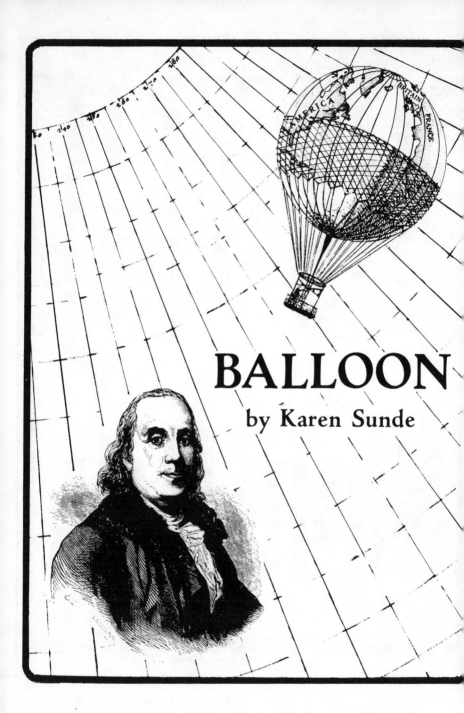

BALLOON

by Karen Sunde

Benjamin Franklin, American Ambassador to Paris during the 18th Century, plays host to his French contemporaries during a festive parlor visit, while the fates of nations hang in the balance.

DEATH in the POT

by Manuel Van Loggem

An English-style thriller with a fascinating plot that takes intricate twists and turns, as a husband and wife try to kill each other off, aided by a mysterious Merchant of Death. Mr. Van Loggem's works have been widely produced throughout Europe.

ESCOFFIER
KING OF CHEFS
by
Owen S. Rackleff

In this one-man show set in a Monte Carlo villa at the end of the last century, the grand master of the kitchen, Escoffier, ponders a glorious return from retirement. In doing so, he relates ancedotes about the famous and shares his mouth-watering recipes with the audience.

SSUMMIT CONFERENCE

ROBERT DAVID MACDONALD

...in The Berlin Chancellery in 1941, the play charts a ficticious encounter ...ween Eva Braun and Clara Petacci. This show ran on London's West End in ...2 with Glenda Jackson.